Funniest Bone Animal Jokes

HYSTERICAL Dog JOKES to Tickle Your FUNNY BONE

Felicia Lowenstein Niven

Enslow Elementary
an imprint of

Enslow Publishers, Inc.
40 Industrial Road
Box 398
Berkeley Heights, NJ 07922
USA

http://www.enslow.com

Enslow Elementary, an imprint of Enslow Publishers, Inc.

Enslow Elementary® is a registered trademark of Enslow Publishers, Inc.

Library of Congress Cataloging-in-Publication Data

Niven, Felicia Lowenstein.
  Hysterical dog jokes to tickle your funny bone / by Felicia Lowenstein Niven.
    pages cm. — (Funniest bone animal jokes)
  Includes index.
  Summary: "Read jokes, limericks, tongue twisters, and knock-knock jokes about dogs and other animals in the canine family. Also find out fun facts about these animals"—Provided by publisher.
  ISBN 978-0-7660-5958-0
  1. Dogs—Juvenile humor. I. Title.
  PN6231.D68N58 2014
  818'.602—dc23
                            2013008791

Future editions:
Paperback ISBN: 978-0-7660-5959-7   EPUB ISBN: 978-0-7660-5960-3
Single-User PDF ISBN: 978-0-7660-5961-0   Multi-User PDF ISBN: 978-0-7660-5962-7

Printed in the United States of America

To Our Readers: We have done our best to make sure all Internet addresses in this book were active and appropriate when we went to press. However, the author and the publisher have no control over and assume no liability for the material available on those Internet sites or on other Web sites they may link to. Any comments or suggestions can be sent by e-mail to comments@enslow.com or to the address on the back cover.

Contents

1 All About Dogs

Where did the dog leave his car?

In the barking lot!

Why don't dogs make good dancers?

They have two left feet!

Knock, knock.

Who's there?

Abbott.

Abbott who?

Abbott time you got a dog!

Dirty dogs don't dig down deep.

4

DID YOU KNOW?

The oldest dog ever recorded lived to be 29 years and 5 months. He was a Queensland heeler breed named Bluey.

What kind of dog loves flowers?

A bud hound!

What's worse than raining cats and dogs?

Hailing taxis!

Dapper dachshunds dance delightedly during December.

What kind of dog sweats?

A hot dog!

What did the dog say when he sat on his doghouse?

"Roof!"

Knock, knock.

Who's there?

Justin.

Justin who?

Justin time to walk the dog!

There once was a puppy named Pat
Who thought he was a bratty cat.
He chased all the mice
And didn't think twice
Until he ran into a rat!

What did the dog say
when he sat on sandpaper?

"Ruff!"

No matter how long I'm away—
A minute, an hour, all day—
One thing is for sure,
Wagging at my door,
My pup says, "You're home! Hip hooray!"

WHAT IS A LIMERICK?

A funny five-line poem in which the first, second, and fifth lines rhyme, and the shorter third and fourth lines rhyme.

Puppy Play

Knock, knock.

Who's there?

Isabel.

Isabel who?

Isabel working? Your dog barked so loud, I couldn't tell.

Playful puppies pounce on plump pillows.

Why is it called a litter of puppies?

Because they mess up the whole house!

FUN FACT

Dalmatian puppies are born completely white. It takes a few weeks for splotches to appear, and then these will darken into dots.

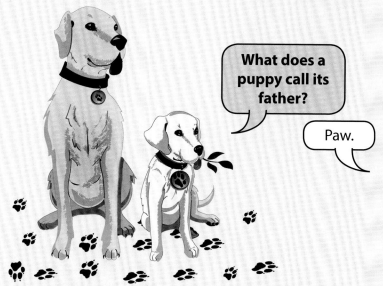

What does a puppy call its father?

Paw.

What do you call young dogs that have just come in from the snow?

Slush puppies!

Knock, knock.

Who's there?

Sara.

Sara who?

Sara vet in the house?

Perky puppies positively prefer postmen.

What's the worst thing about getting a young dog?

The pup-PEE!

What do you call a dog who picks on puppies?

A bully dog!

Limerick

What kind of a pup would you most like to choose?
Maybe a dog breed that got good reviews?
Whether short, sleek, or scruffy,
Tall, broad, or puffy,
With so many breeds, you simply can't lose!

Where do you usually find puppies?

It all depends on where you lose them!

Limerick

The puppy that wanted to play
Chased everything out of its way.
Only the cat
Refused to scat,
And stayed in the spot where she lay.

FUN FACT

Puppies are born with their eyes closed. They won't open them until they are about two weeks old. That's because their eyes are still developing.

③ Purebreds

When is a dog not a dog?

When it is pure bread!

What breed of dog loves to take a bath?

A shampoodle.

What kind of dog does Dracula have?

A bloodhound!

DID YOU KNOW?

Long ago in the Far East, Pekingese and Japanese Chin breeds were considered so special that they had their own servants.

What do you call a pit bull wearing earmuffs?

Anything you want; he can't hear you.

Chilly Chihuahuas choose cheerful chintz prints.

When is a brown dog not a brown dog?

When it's a greyhound.

Which dog will laugh at any joke?

A chi-ha-ha!

Limerick

There was a young beagle named Fred,
Who usually did what Sam said.
But when Sam said, "Stay!"
Fred thought it was "Play,"
And he pulled Sam's socks off instead!

Princely poodles prance perfectly.

What kind of dog can use the phone?

A dial-matian!

Limerick

Said the poodle to the groomer, "Alright,
I've got a Hollywood party tonight.
A designer shampoo
And a pretty hairdo—
Bows and nail polish, I'll look out of sight."

14

WHAT IS A TONGUE TWISTER?

A series of fun words with similar sounds that can be hard to say out loud.

Mixed Breeds

What do you get when you cross a sheepdog with a rose?

A collie-flower!

Knock, knock.

Who's there?

Hatch.

Hatch who?

Bless you. Are you allergic to dogs?

What do you get when you cross a dog with a lion?

A really scared mail carrier!

No matter what the breed, all dogs have 321 bones and 42 permanent teeth.

What do you get when you cross a dog with a phone?

A golden receiver!

What do you get when you cross a frog and a dog?

A croaker spaniel!

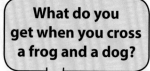

What do you get when you cross a cocker spaniel, a poodle, and a rooster?

A cockerpoodledoo!

What do you get when you cross a dog with a cheetah?

A dog that chases cars and catches them!

17

Like a Doberman, Drake liked to strut;
But the tail he had was anything but.
Like a Lab, he was jolly,
And smart as a collie.
Have you guessed that Drake was a mutt?

My mad mutt Max
makes mice move
mysteriously.

Knock, knock.

Who's there?

Freeze.

Freeze who?

Freeze a jolly
good doggie, which
nobody can deny!

Limerick

I'm trying to give my puppy a name.
Just calling her Dog or Pup is too lame.
I may be mistaken,
The good names are taken—
She's too special to sound just the same!

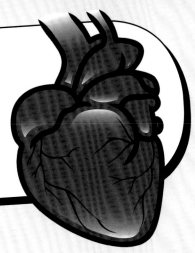

FUN FACT

A dog's heart beats between 70 and 120 times per minute. A healthy human heart beats 70 to 80 times a minute.

What do you get when you cross a Labrador retriever with a tortoise?

An animal that goes to the newsstand and comes back with last week's paper!

Denny, a dachshund Dalmatian, dated a Doberman dingo.

5 Wild Dogs

What did one coyote say to the other?

Let's go catch some fast food!

Limerick

Coyotes like to howl at the moon
Whether it's March, April, May, or June.
The pack gathers round
To hear the great sound.
You might say that they play Name That Tune!

FUN FACT

Coyotes sing to each other. They use these howling "songs" as a way to communicate with other coyotes.

What do you call a lost wolf?

A where-wolf!

What did one wolf say to another wolf?

Howl's it going?

DID YOU KNOW?

A wolf eats about 20 pounds of food at a meal. That's the same as a person eating 80 hamburgers!

How do coyotes bake a cake?

From scratch!

Clever coyotes catch crazy colored cats!

The color of wolves is a sight.
They can be black, gray, red, or white.
But when they appear,
Whether far or near,
You'd better remember, they bite!

Why wouldn't the wolf eat the clown?

It would make him feel funny.

Knock, knock.

Who's there?

Ron.

Ron who?

Ron a little faster! There's a coyote after us!

23

6 Man's Best Friend

What did the cowboy say when his dog ran away?

Well, doggone!

What kind of dog does a mad scientist have?

A laboratory retriever!

DID YOU KNOW?

A dog's sense of smell is at least 14 times better than a person's. That is why they can sniff out dinner even if they're not in the kitchen!

25

Paula's puffy puppy plowed through the scrumptious pumpkin pie.

Limerick

Fetch is the name of a popular game.
You throw the stick or the toy where you aim.
But just be prepared,
It never ends there:
You'll have to do this again and again!

Knock, knock.

Who's there?

Oliver.

Oliver who?

Oliver sudden my dog went crazy!

In Alaska, the husky dogs are king.
Strength and endurance to the race they bring.
In the Iditarod
They pull sleds as a squad,
Then they celebrate for the rest of spring!

Why did the man bring his dog to the railroad station?

Because he wanted to train him!

Where do dogsled racers train their team?

In the mush room!

27

Dog's Best Enemies

Knock, knock.

Who's there?

Police.

Police who?

Police open the door! I'm a cat and there's a dog out here!

What did one flea say to the other?

"Should we walk or take the dog?"

DID YOU KNOW?

Cats have powerful night vision. While they can't see any better in the dark than humans do, they can see much better in dim light. Dogs can also see better at night than humans can—but probably not as well as cats.

FLEA MARKET

What place should you never take a dog?

A flea market!

Limerick

On a dog, a couple of fleas
Were thrown on account of a sneeze.
They scrambled around,
Bounced up off the ground,
Then grabbed the dog's fur near its knees!

How do fleas travel from place to place?

By itch-hiking!

What did the dog say to the flea?

"Quit bugging me!"

29

Knock, knock.

Who's there?

Fleas.

Fleas who?

Fleased to meet you!

What state has the most cats and dogs?

Petsylvania!

Why did the cat run from the tree?

It was afraid of its bark!

Limerick
There once was a dog named Matt
Who thought that he was a cat.
When it came to how
He couldn't meow,
Well, that was the end of that.

What animals do caterpillars fear the most?

Dog-erpillars!

FUN FACT

Fleas can jump 30,000 times in a row without stopping!

What is a cat's way of keeping law and order?

Claw enforcement!

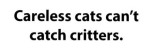

Careless cats can't catch critters.

Fleas find furry friends fantastic!

Knock, knock.

Who's there?

Wendy.

Wendy who?

Wendy dinner bell rings, the dog's the first one there.

How are dogs like phones?

They both have collar ID.

TAG DAY

How do you keep a dog from barking in your front yard?

Put it in your backyard!

When does a dog go moo?

When it is learning a new language!

Rory the Rottweiler ran races rapidly.

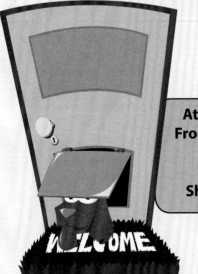

Limerick
At our house, we all have a chore,
From cooking to mopping the floor.
The dog does her share
With her normal flair:
She greets everyone at the door.

Knock, knock.

Who's there?

Annie.

Annie who?

Annie thing you can do, my dog can do, too.

Seven sleeping shepherds snore shrilly.

What did the man say after he gave his dog some glue?

"Stick 'em, Fido!"

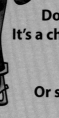

Limerick

Dogs love to go out for a walk.
It's a chance to sniff 'round and gawk—
Or find a rabbit
And then try to grab it,
Or sit still and watch like a hawk.

9 It's a Dog's Life

What is a dog's favorite city?

New Yorkie!

What dog keeps the best time?

A watch dog!

Why are Dalmatians no good at hide-and-seek?

They're always spotted!

36

Dogs are not color blind. They just see fewer colors than we do. Red is hard for dogs to see, but blue is easy.

What does a dog become after it is six years old?

Seven years old!

Knock, knock.

Who's there?

Canoe.

Canoe who?

Canoe help me with the dog?

What is taller when it sits down than when it stands up?

A dog!

37

Knock, knock.

Who's there?

Dozen.

Dozen who?

Dozen anyone want this cute doggie?

What did the dog say when he finally caught his tail?

"This is the end."

Lily the Lhasa liked licking lollipops!

Limerick

It's playtime for dogs at the park.
They all seem to be testing their bark.
Running round and round,
Rolling on the ground,
They'll all want to stay out past dark!

FUN FACT

The basenji breed is the only kind of dog that cannot bark.

Ten tiny terriers scurry hurriedly.

Limerick

Biscuits are yummy, you see.
Sometimes I get two or three.
But my tastes are bold,
And the truth be told,
I much prefer fricassee.

What is the first trick a politician's dog learns?

How to shake hands.

Meddlesome mastiffs are mischief-makers.

What did the hungry Dalmatian say after his meal?

"That hit the spots!"

Salukis are also known as gazelle hounds or Persian greyhounds. Like greyhounds, when salukis run at full speed, all four paws are off the ground at the same time.

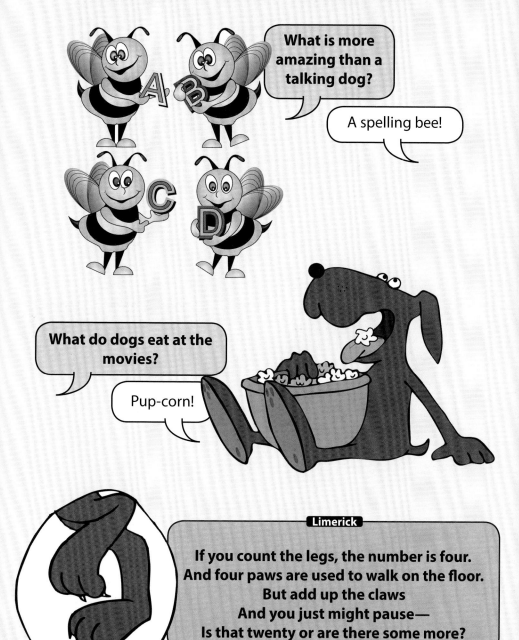

What is more amazing than a talking dog?

A spelling bee!

What do dogs eat at the movies?

Pup-corn!

Limerick

If you count the legs, the number is four.
And four paws are used to walk on the floor.
But add up the claws
And you just might pause—
Is that twenty or are there some more?

Knock, knock.

Who's there?

Arthur.

Arthur who?

Arthur any more dog biscuits?

Knock, knock.

Who's there?

Dewey.

Dewey who?

Dewey have to keep telling these dog jokes?

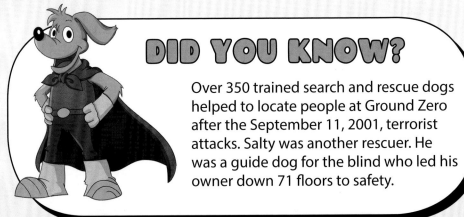

DID YOU KNOW?

Over 350 trained search and rescue dogs helped to locate people at Ground Zero after the September 11, 2001, terrorist attacks. Salty was another rescuer. He was a guide dog for the blind who led his owner down 71 floors to safety.

FUN FACT

Rin Tin Tin was the first dog to become a Hollywood star. He actually signed his movie contracts with his paw print!

How does a dog stop a DVD?

It presses the paws button!

Six spunky salukis sit silently in succession.

Limerick
A talented dog named Spot
Knew how to untangle a knot.
He was so quick,
The knot he'd pick
And never ever get caught.

Make a Dog Breed Book

Here's What You Will Need:

- paper
- colored markers
- glue stick
- scissors
- stapler

Directions:

1. Find pictures in old magazines or online of different dog breeds that interest you.

2. Cut out or print the pictures.

3. Use the glue stick to attach each picture to a larger piece of paper.

4. Look up an interesting fact about each dog breed and write it under the picture. Or you could write a joke about each one!

   What kind of dogs like to do science experiments?
   Lab-rador retrievers!

   When it rains cats and dogs, be careful not to step in the poodles!

5. Draw a cover for your book.

6. Staple all the pages together.

Words to Know

breed—A group of animals that share traits that make them different from other animals of the same kind. For example, Dobermans, German shepherds, and poodles are three breeds of dogs.

chintz—A cotton fabric with patterns such as flowers, often used for curtains and furniture covers.

fricassee—A meal made of meat cooked in white sauce.

groomer—A person who helps an animal stay clean and neat by bathing and brushing it.

Iditarod—A long-distance dogsled race held every year in Alaska.

joke—Something said to make people laugh.

limerick—A funny five-line poem in which the first, second, and fifth lines rhyme, and the shorter third and fourth lines rhyme.

purebred—An animal whose parents and ancestors come from the same breed.

tongue twister—A series of fun words with similar sounds that can be hard to say out loud.

Read More

Books

Dahl, Michael. *The Funny Farm: Jokes About Dogs, Cats, Ducks, Snakes, Bears and Other Animals*. Mankato, Minn.: Picture Window Books, 2010.

Elliott, Rob. *Zoolarious Animal Jokes for Kids*. Ada, Mich.: Revell, 2012.

Lederer, Richard, and Jim Ertner. *Super Funny Animal Jokes (Animal Cracker Uppers)*. Portland, Oreg.: Marion Street Press, 2011.

National Geographic. *Kids Just Joking: 300 Hilarious Jokes, Tricky Tongue Twisters, and Ridiculous Riddles*. Des Moines, Iowa: National Geographic Children's Books, 2012.

Internet Addresses

Animal Planet: Dogs 101
http://animal.discovery.com/tv-shows/dogs-101

PBS: Extraordinary Dogs
http://www.pbs.org/wnet/extraordinarydogs/

Index